In January, 1990, Quilt in a Day friends met to plan a year of quiltmaking. They brought ideas, quilt block patterns, recipes, but most of all they brought the joy of old-time quilting get-togethers.

Although Eleanor Burns hosted these block parties each month, it was the women themselves who set the guidelines and selected the block patterns that were to become this sampler quilt.

One of the guidelines was to agree collectively on a "challenge fabric." Once that decision was made, each quiltmaker then had the freedom to use that challenge fabric as an inspiration to select other fabrics.

The challenge fabric was a multi-colored floral on a black background. With that as a starting point, the task then became to choose two color families. And with those two colors in mind, they began searching for specific fabrics in three values--light, medium and dark.

As the year progressed they eagerly made their blocks, finding that Eleanor's easy construction methods often took less than an hour each. Quarterly they sewed together three blocks, some machine quilting the rows onto batting, while others chose to layer the entire quilt at year's end.

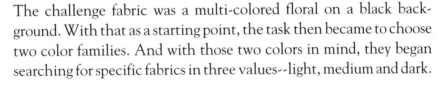

The resulting diversity of their beautiful quilts is a credit to their creative spirit. And as with all quilts, they serve as a reminder of times past. In this case, their quilts are memories of the companionship, creativity, and happy times of their meetings.

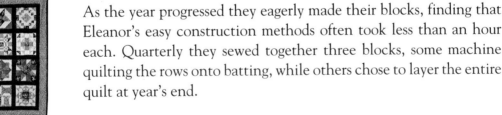

1

Yardage

Twelve 12" Blocks Approximate Finished Size: 57" x 70"

Select a good quality of 100% cotton from two different color families that compliment each other. From each of these families, choose a light, medium, and a dark. In addition, select any coordinating scraps from your stash.

When choosing your fabrics for each new block during the year, select fabrics different from those in the adjacent completed blocks.

Light

Choose either one light that works for both families, or a second one for variety. The light should be a solid as muslin, appear solid from a distance, or be a small scaled print.

1 1/2 yds. of one light or
3/4 yd. each of two different lights

Medium and Dark

From each of these families, select a medium and a dark. In addition, vary the size of the prints, as a large scaled multi-colored print, a medium scaled print, a small scaled print, and one that appears solid from a distance. Mediums and darks can be used interchangeably in the blocks as long as there is the desired contrast.

3/4 yd. each of two different mediums
3/4 yd. each of two different darks

Lattice

Purchase a solid color of 100% cotton that coordinates with your two main colors. Consider making the fabric selection after several blocks are completed and can be placed on the choices.

1 1/8 yds.
Cut (12) strips 3" wide by 45" long.
From these,

Cut (3) long strips into
(8) 3" x 12 1/2" strips.
Leave (9) strips 3" x 45".

Border

Square off the selvage edges and sew the short ends into one long strip. Clip the threads and press the seams to one side. The border strip is ready to be cut to needed widths and lengths for either "finish."

1 1/4 yds.
Cut (7) 6" x 45" strips.

Backing

Remove the selvages, and sew those edges together. The seam appears horizontally across the center back of the finished quilt.

3 1/2 yds.
Cut into (2) equal pieces.

Bonded Batting

Select a thick 8 oz. bonded batting for a quick turn finish. Select a lightweight 3 oz. bonded batting for a machine quilted finish with binding.

72" x 90"

Binding for Machine Quilted Finish Only

Square off the selvage edges, assembly- line sew the short ends into one long strip, and clip the threads. Press lengthwise, wrong sides together.

2/3 yd.
Cut (7) 3" x 45" strips.

Supplies Needed

Industrial size rotary cutter with fresh blade, gridded cutting mat, 6" x 24" ruler, 12 1/2" Square Up, 6" square ruler, marking pencil or chalk, magnetic seam guide, neutral thread, nylon filament invisible thread, extra long quilters pins.

Additional Supplies for:

Unquilted Finish: curved needle, embroidery floss

Quilted Finish: walking foot attachment, (50) 1" safety pins and a grapefruit spoon to aid pinning

How to Use the Quilters' Almanac

Each block has two pages of instruction.

The first page

The first page shows a color photograph as well as a smaller block pattern for coloring. The cutting chart on this page color codes the suggested number of light, medium and dark fabrics to correlate with the photograph. This tells which of your fabrics to cut for specific parts of the block. The small color patches to the right of the brackets show what the bracketed fabric pieces will make once the sewing is completed.

For instance in January:

5" x 10" light

5" x 10" medium

4

Once sewn this . . . . . yields this

- Select a light and a medium fabric.

- Press right sides together with light on top, lining up selvage edges on a corner of the fabric.

- With the 12 1/2" square ruler, layer cut pieces slightly larger than 5" x 10".

- Turn the pieces, and cut to exact size of 5" x 10".

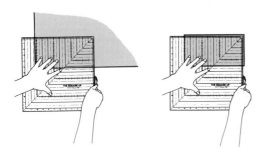

- Pieces cut right sides together are now ready for sewing instructions on the second page.

Use the 6" square for pieces smaller than 6". For several squares, cut a strip that measurement first, and then cut the squares.

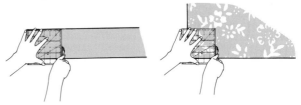

To do "fussy cuts," center the design within the square.

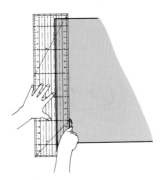

When cutting rectangles and squares, cut from one side of the 45" wide fabric. Cut strips from the opposite side of the fabric with the 6" x 24" ruler.

- Straighten the edge.

- Move your ruler over until the ruler lines are at the freshly cut edge. Carefully and accurately line up and cut the strips at the measurements given.

The second page

The second page gives the instructions for making the block parts from the pieces just cut. Each patch is color coded to indicate which fabrics to use in the step-by-step directions.

Mark the "square lines" on the back of the layered rectangles or squares using the lines on the gridded cutting mat.

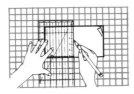
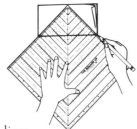
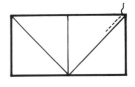

Use the 12 1/2" square ruler for marking diagonal lines.

- **Use an accurate and consistent 1/4" seam allowance.** Sew a few stitches and measure. If necessary, make adjustments by changing your needle position, or your foot until your seam is 1/4".

- **Use 15 stitches per inch**, or 2 to 2.5 on machines with stitch selections from 1 to 4.

Wandering Star

January

Easy block

made by Pat Wetzel

Choose a light,
medium,
and two darks.

Create your own block.

Cutting Instructions

Layer Cut Right Sides Together

(1) 5" x 10" light

(1) 5" x 10" medium

4

(1) 5" square light

(1) 5" square first dark

2

(1) 5" square light

(1) 5" square second dark

2

Cut in Fourths on the Diagonals ⊠

(1) 5 1/2" square first dark

(1) 5 1/2" square second dark

1

Discard 2 of each.

**Making
Four**

**Making
Two**

1. Draw on a 5" square line.

2. Draw on diagonal lines. Pin.

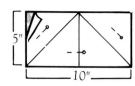

3. Draw on diagonal lines. Pin.

4. Sew a **1/4" seam** on both sides of the diagonal lines. Start at *. Press.

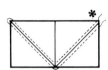 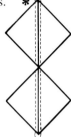

5. Cut apart on all lines.

6. Press the seams to the darker side.

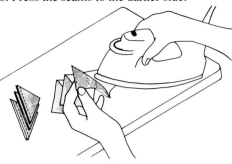

7. Square to 4 1/2".

If the piece is less than 4 1/2", the seam allowance was too wide. Resew with a narrower seam and remove the original stitches.

**Making
One**

1. Lay out four pieces in this order:

2. Flip the pieces on the right to the pieces on the left.

3. Assembly-line sew.

4. Open, turn, and flip right sides together. Sew, matching the seam in the center, and pushing the seams in opposite directions.

5. Press and square to 4 1/2".

**Sewing
the Block
Together**

1. Lay out the pieces.

2. Flip the second vertical row right sides together to the first.

3. Assembly-line sew, matching the pieces and backstitching the outside edges. Do not clip apart.

4. Flip the third vertical row right sides together to the second. Assembly-line sew.

5. Sew the horizontal rows, pushing the seams in opposite directions, toward the dark when possible.

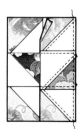

Wandering Star is the first block in the first row.
Set aside until the March block is completed.

January

Sunday	Monday	Tuesday	Wednesday
☐	☐	☐	☐
☐	☐	☐	☐
☐	☐	☐	☐
☐	☐	☐	☐
☐	☐	☐	☐

4 eggs
1 cup mayonnaise
1 1/2 cups shredded cheddar cheese
3/4 cup diced, cooked chicken
10 oz pkg frozen chopped broccoli,
    thawed and drained

3 chopped green onions
1 Tbl lemon juice
one 9" frozen deep dish pie crust

Chicken Divan Quiche
Debbie Smith

Mix all ingredients together and pour into pie crust. Bake 375 ° 45 minutes until puffy and golden brown and knife inserted in center comes out clean. Try any of these combinations: spinach, mixed vegetables, mushrooms, almonds, sausage, ham and swiss cheese.

Thursday	Friday	Saturday
☐	☐	☐
☐	☐	☐
☐	☐	☐
☐	☐	☐
☐	☐	☐

Tips

Having trouble pulling a curved needle through thick batting? Running the needle through your hair gives it a thin coating of oil. Grip it tighter by wrapping a balloon around the needle or wear a "rubber finger."

Make it a practice to sign the back of your quilts. Include your city, the date it was completed, the pattern name and any interesting information about the project.

Mackie

Road to the White House

February

Easy block   made by Waltraut Meyer

Choose a light,
two mediums,
and two darks.

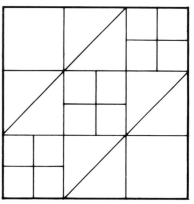

Create your own block.

Cutting Instructions

Layer Cut Right Sides Together

(1) 5" x 10" first medium

(1) 5" x 10" second medium

4

(1) 2 1/2" x 18" strip light

(1) 2 1/2" x 18" strip first dark

3

Layer Cut

(2) 4 1/2" second dark squares

2

Making Four

1. Draw on a 5" square line.
2. Draw on diagonal lines. Pin.

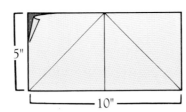

3. Sew a **1/4" seam** on both sides of the diagonal lines. Press.

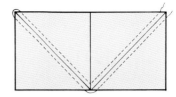

4. Cut apart on all lines.
5. Press the seams to the darker side.
6. Square to 4 1/2".

Making Three

1. Sew the strips together.
2. Press the seam to the dark side.
3. Cut into (2) 9" pieces.

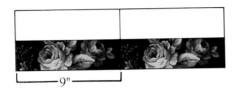

4. Flip right sides together with the darks opposite each other.
5. Cut into (3) 2 1/2" sections.

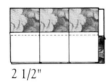

2 1/2"

6. Wiggle-match the center seam. Assembly-line sew.

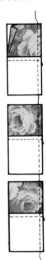

7. Press and square to 4 1/2".

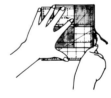 

Sewing the Block Together

Variation: Notice that the quilt on the cover has a "light" road. Experiment with yours.

1. Lay out the pieces.
2. Sew the vertical rows
3. Sew the horizontal rows.

Road to the White House is the middle block in the first row.

Set aside until the March block is completed.

February

As ye sew, so shall ye rip.

Sunday	Monday	Tuesday	Wednesday

2 cups sugar
16 large marshmallows
1 sm can evaporated milk
1 stick margarine
12 oz chocolate chips
1 tsp vanilla

Sweetheart Fudge
Dana Butler

Place sugar, marshmallows, and milk in large pan. Bring to boil over low heat, stirring constantly. Remove from heat and add margarine, chips, and vanilla. Stir until creamy. Add walnuts if desired. Pour into greased 9 inch square pan. Refrigerate until solid.

Thursday	Friday	Saturday

Tips

Busy sewing for the holidays? When having difficulty finding a color of thread to match your fabric, use a light grey thread. Light grey seems to blend well with many prints.

Wind extra bobbins when starting a project to keep up the momentum. Use the same thread in the top and bobbin. Each time you change your bobbin, dust out the bobbin case with a can of condensed air.

Clean and oil your sewing machine regularly and change needles often. Attention to maintenance pays off.

Keep a pointed sewing tool or seam ripper next to your sewing machine. Use it to push stubborn seam allowances flat.

Irish Chain

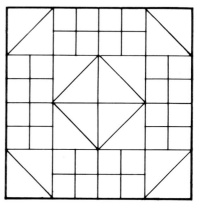

March

Intermediate block

made by Eleanor Burns

Choose a light,
two mediums,
and a dark.

Create your own block.

Cutting Instructions

Layer Cut Right Sides Together

(1) 4" x 8" light
(1) 4" x 8" first medium
 4

(1) 4" x 8" light
(1) 4" x 8" dark
 4

(1) 2 1/8" x 40" strip light
(1) 2 1/8" x 40" strip second medium
 8

Making Four

1. Draw on a 4" square line.

2. Draw on diagonal lines. Pin.

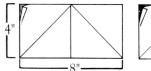
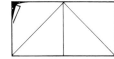

4"

8"

3. Sew a **1/4" seam** on both sides of the diagonal lines. Press.

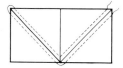
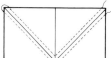

4. Cut apart on all lines.

5. Press the seams to the darker side.

6. Square to 3 1/2".

Making Eight

1. Sew the strips together.

2. Press the seam to the medium side.

3. Cut into (2) 20" pieces.

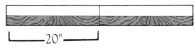

20"

4. Flip right sides together with the mediums opposite each other.

2 1/8"

5. Cut into (8) 2 1/8" sections.

6. Wiggle-match the center seam. Assembly-line sew.

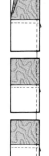

7. Press and square to 3 1/2".

Sewing the Block Together

1. Lay out the pieces.

2. Sew the vertical rows.

3. Sew the horizontal rows.

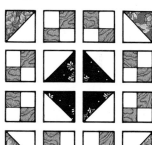

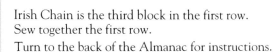

Variation made by Betty Miller

Variation made by Waltraut Meyer

Irish Chain is the third block in the first row.
Sew together the first row.
Turn to the back of the Almanac for instructions.

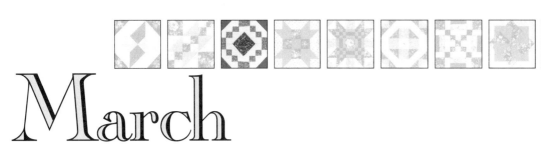

March

Sunday	Monday	Tuesday	Wednesday

3 carrots, cut in 3-inch pieces
2-3 medium onions, quartered
3 pound corned beef brisket
1-2 cups water

Corned Beef and Cabbage
Pat Wetzel

Put all ingredients in crockpot in order listed. Cover. Set at Low for 10 to 12 hours. (High: 5 to 6 hours). Add 1/2 head **cabbage** wedges and 3 quartered **potatoes** to liquid, pushing down to moisten, after 6 hours on Low (or 3 hours on High). Season to Taste.

Tips

What's a lap robe called that's long enough to cover toes on a cold day? Piggies in a Blanket

Position your patches on a piece of flannel board as you work. Back up and squint at your quilt as it progresses. If possible, view the quilt in progress from a second floor balcony. Snap poloroid photos while changing block layouts to help pinpoint your favorite one.

Thursday	Friday	Saturday

Farmer's Daughter

Intermediate block

made by Pat Wetzel

April

Choose a light,
medium,
and dark.

Create your own block.

Cutting Instructions

Layer Cut Right Sides Together

(1) 7" square light

(1) 7" square medium

8

Layer Cut

(4) 3" squares dark

 4

(5) 3" squares medium

 5

(8) 3" squares light

 8

16

Making Eight

1. Draw on 3 1/2" square lines.
2. Draw on diagonal lines. Pin.

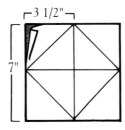

3. Sew a **1/4" seam** on both sides of the diagonal lines. Press.

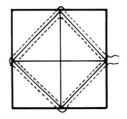

4. Cut apart on all lines.
5. Press the seams to the medium side.
6. Square to 3".

Sewing the Block Together

1. Lay out the pieces.

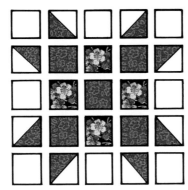

2. Sew the vertical rows with a 1/4" seam allowance plus two threads. A 3/8" seam allowance is too wide.

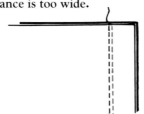

3. Press and measure the top row. If the measurement is 12 1/2" or the same as previous blocks, continue using this same seam allowance for this block. If the block is more than 12 1/2", take a deeper seam; if it is less, take a narrower seam and remove the first stitching.

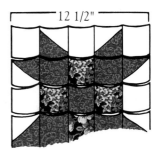

4. Sew the horizontal rows.

This same seam allowance plus two threads technique applies to May and June blocks, also.

Variation by Carmen Gil

Variation by Marvie Colton

Farmer's Daughter is the first block in the second row.

Set aside until the June block is completed.

April

When life gives you scraps, make quilts.

Sunday	Monday	Tuesday	Wednesday

2 cups boiling water
6 cups bran
1 cup shortening (melted)
5 cups flour
3 cups sugar or less

5 tsp soda
2 tsp salt
4 eggs, beaten
1 qt buttermilk

Six Weeks Bran Muffins
Eleanor Burns

Mix in large covered container. Pour boiling water over 2 cups bran. Add melted shortening. Mix. Sift together dry ingredients. Add all ingredients together and mix. Pour batter into greased muffin tins. Bake at 400 ° for 20 minutes. Makes 4 doz. delicious muffins! For variety, add raisins, nuts, dates, apple bits, mashed banana. May be stored in refrigerator and used when needed for up to 6 weeks.

Tips

Check a possible striped mitered corner by placing a mirror at the 45° angle on the border stripe.

A multi-lens reflector will show one block multiple times through 25 rectangular lenses.

Be careful not to run over pins with your rotary cutter. When you need to replace the blade, carefully lay the parts out in order as you disassemble it, so parts can be reassembled correctly. If your rotary cutter is no longer gliding freely, lubricate it lightly with a drop of sewing machine oil.

Thursday	Friday	Saturday

Young Man's Fancy

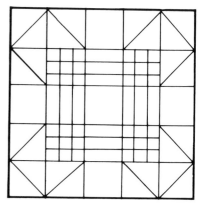

Advanced block

made by Mildred Andres

Choose a light,
two mediums,
and two darks.

Create your own block.

Cutting Instructions

Layer Cut Right Sides Together

(1) 7" square light
(1) 7" square first dark
⎤ 8

(1) 3 1/2" x 7" light
(1) 3 1/2" x 7" first medium
⎤ 4

Layer Cut

(2) 1 3/8" x 45" strips second medium
(2) 1 3/8" x 45" strips second dark
⎤

+

4

(4) 3" squares first medium
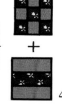
4

(1) 3" square first dark

1

Making

Eight

and

Four

1. Draw on 3 1/2" square lines.

2. Draw on diagonal lines. Pin.

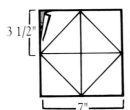 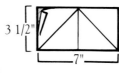

3. Sew a **1/4" seam** on both sides of the diagonal lines. Press.

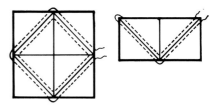

4. Cut apart on all lines.

5. Press the seams to the darker side.

6. Square to 3".

Making

Four

1. Cut a 14" piece from each 45" strip.

2. Lay out strips. Discard extras.

3. Sew together.

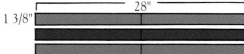

4. Press the seams to the darker sides. The sewn together strips should measure no less than 3".

5. Flip the shorter set of strips right sides together to the longer set, and nestle the seams together.

6. Cut into (4) 1 3/8" sections. These layered sections are ready for sewing.

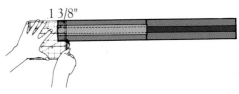

7. Remove the shorter set excess and cut from it an additional (4) 1 3/8" sections.

8. Assembly-line sew the layered 1 3/8" sections. Wiggle-match the seams in the center.

9. Add a single section, completing each nine-patch.

10. Press the seams to the dark side.

11. Cut (4) 3" sections.

12. Square to 3", trimming edges equally.

Sewing

the Block

Together

1. Lay out the pieces.

2. **Sew the vertical and horizontal rows with a 1/4" seam allowance plus two threads.**

Variation: Turn medium corners in.

Young Man's Fancy is the middle block in the second row.

Set aside until the June block is completed.

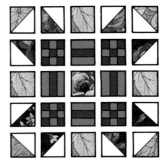

May

May your sorrows be patched, and your joys be quilted.

Sunday	Monday	Tuesday	Wednesday

1 pound ground beef
2 onions chopped
1/2 cup Minute Rice
1 can cream of chicken soup
1 can cream of mushroom soup

1 1/2 cups water
1/4 tsp pepper
1/8 cup soy sauce (optional)
Small can Chow Mein noodles

Mother's Day Casserole
LuAnn Stout

Brown meat and onions. Add remaining ingredients except noodles. Pour into large casserole dish. Cover and bake at 350° for 30 minutes. Last 10 minutes cover with Chow Mein noodles. Bake longer if regular rice is used.

Tips

Magic with Mirrors
Check the contrast in your block by viewing it through a mirror at the opposite end of the room.

When repeat blocks are set together without lattice, interesting secondary patterns appear. To see how multiples of one block look, stand two mirrors at a right angle next to the block. Four blocks will magically appear! Try it with this month's block. You may want to make a quilt with just this pattern.

Thursday	Friday	Saturday

Wedding Ring

Intermediate block

made by Eleanor Burns

Choose a light,
two mediums,
and two darks.

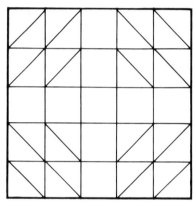

Create your own block.

Cutting Instructions

Layer Cut Right Sides Together

(1) 3 1/2" x 7" light

(1) 3 1/2" x 7" first medium

 4

(1) 3 1/2" x 7" light

(1) 3 1/2" x 7" first dark

 4

(1) 7" square light

(1) 7" square second dark

 8

Layer Cut

(5) 3" squares light

 5

(4) 3" squares second medium

 4

24

Making

Four

and

Eight

1. Draw on 3 1/2" square lines.

2. Draw on diagonal lines. Pin.

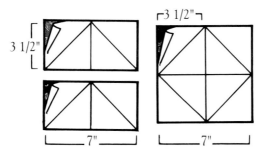

3. Sew a **1/4" seam** on both sides of the diagonal lines. Press.

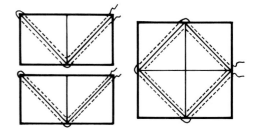

4. Cut apart on all lines.

5. Press the seams to the darker side.

6. Square to 3".

Sewing the Block Together

1. Lay out the pieces.

2. **Sew the vertical and horizontal rows with a 1/4" seam allowance plus two threads.**

Variation by Carolyn Smith

Variation by Mildred Andres

Wedding Ring is the third block in the second row.

Sew together the second row.

Turn to the back of the Almanac for instructions.

June

Sunday	Monday	Tuesday	Wednesday

1 small pkg slivered almonds
2 Tbl sesame seeds
2-3 Chicken Breasts, cooked and shredded
1 medium cabbage, shredded fine
4 green onions, with tops, chopped
1 pkg Ramen noodles with seasoning, uncooked

Dressing:
3 Tbl Japanese rice wine vinegar
1 Tbl red wine vinegar
1 Tbl sesame seed oil
1/4 cup salad oil
3 Tbl sugar
1 tsp salt

Chinese Chicken & Cabbage Salad

Marcia Lasher

Toast the almonds and sesame seeds under the broiler. One hour before serving, mix together all ingredients except the Ramen noodles. Just before serving, break up the noodles in the package and toss with the salad.

Thursday	Friday	Saturday
☐	☐	☐
☐	☐	☐
☐	☐	☐
☐	☐	☐
☐	☐	☐

Tips

A dry, thin sliver of soap is perfect for marking dark fabrics.

Take snapshots of your finished quilts in order to remember the ones that will have new homes.

To remove folds from a newly hung quilt, lightly mist it with a spray bottle of warm water.

27

Independence Square

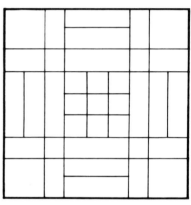

Intermediate block

made by Luckie Yasukochi

July

Choose a light,
two mediums,
and two darks.

Create your own block.

Cutting Instructions

(1) 3 1/4" x 14" strip first dark

(1) 1 7/8" x 14" strip light

4

(1) 3 1/4" x 9" strip light

(1) 1 7/8" x 9" strip first medium

4

Layer Cut

(1) 1 7/8" x 19" strip second dark

(1) 1 7/8" x 19" strip second medium

(1) 1 7/8" x 19" strip light

4

(1) 1 7/8" x 5" strip light

(2) 1 7/8" x 5" strips first dark

(2) 1 7/8" squares light

(1) 1 7/8" square first dark

1

28

Making Four

1. Sew the 14" strips together.
2. Press the seam to the dark side.
3. Cut (4) 3 1/8" sections.

└ 3 1/8" ┘

4. Sew the 9" strips together.
5. Press the seam to the medium side.
6. Cut (4) 1 7/8" sections.

1 7/8"

Making Four

7. Assembly-line sew the two sections together. Press.

3 1/8"   1 7/8"

8. Square to 4 1/2", trimming from the dark/light sides only.

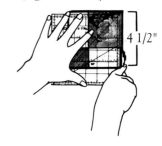

4 1/2"

Making Four

1. Sew the 19" strips together.
2. Press the seams to the dark side.

   Measure the width. If it is more than 4 1/2", sliver trim the dark strip.

3. Cut (4) 4 1/2" sections.

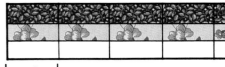

└ 4 1/2" ┘

Making One

1. Sew the 5" strips together.
2. Press the seams to the dark sides.
3. Cut (2) 1 7/8" sections.

1 7/8"

4. Sew the (3) 1 7/8" squares together.

5. Press the seams to the dark side.
6. Sew into a nine-patch.
7. Square to 4 1/2" trimming edges equally.

Sewing the Block Together

1. Lay out the pieces.
2. Sew the vertical rows, carefully matching the seams.
3. Sew the horizontal rows.

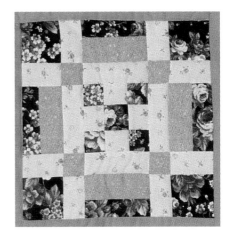

Independence Square is the first block in the third row.

Set aside until the September block is completed.

Variation made by Evelyn Stone

July

Life is a patchwork of friends.

Sunday	Monday	Tuesday	Wednesday

2 small strawberry jello packages
1 20 oz can crushed pineapple
2 10 oz boxes frozen strawberries
   with sugar
1 crushed banana
8 oz sour cream

Thursday	Friday	Saturday
☐	☐	☐
☐	☐	☐
☐	☐	☐
☐	☐	☐
☐	☐	☐

Fourth of July Strawberry Jello

Gail Jakimzak

Mix 2 packages jello with 1 1/2 cups hot water. Add drained pineapple, strawberries and banana. Mix together in bowl. Pour half of mixture into 9 1/2 x 11 inch baking dish. Let mixture firm in refrigerator for 1/2 hour or so, then spread sour cream on top evenly and add the other half of mixture on top and keep in refrigerator.

Tips

Teach your cat to sleep on a towel to keep hairs off your quilt...or better yet, make a kitty quilt!

Stubborn stains on your quilt? Fresh blood stains can be removed by "sponging" saliva into them. Peroxide dropped on the spot and rinsed immediately will also remove blood. Spray hair spray on ink from a ball point pen and then spot wash.

All woven through your quilt,
Are the best days of your life.
The high days. The holidays.
The days of joy and strife.

Tumbleweed

Advanced block

made by Joy Harvey

August

Choose a light,
medium,
and dark.

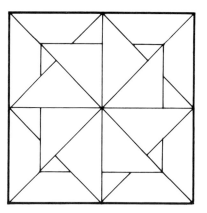

Create your own block.

Cutting Instructions

Layer Cut Right Sides Together

(2) 2 1/4" x 30" strips medium
(2) 2 1/4" x 30" strips light

8

Cut

(4) 2 3/4" squares dark

4

Cut in Fourths on the Diagonals ☒

(1) 7 1/2" square medium

4

(1) 7 1/2" square dark

4

Making Four

1. Sew the two sets of strips.
2. Press the seams to the darker side.

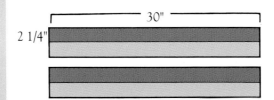

2 1/4"

3. Pin four dark triangles right sides together to one strip. Line up the bottom of the triangle with the bottom of the strip.

4. Stitch.
5. Cut out the four pieces, using the triangles as the pattern.
6. Press the seams to the darker side.
7. Trim off the tips.

Making Four

1. On the **right side** of each medium triangle, draw a line 2" in from the right end.

2. Position the 2 3/4" dark square right sides together to the triangle on the line.
3. Assembly-line sew.

2 3/4"

4. Fold and press the dark square back over the medium triangle.

5. From the wrong side, trim.
6. Pin right sides together to the strip. Carefully match and pin the marked dot 1/4" in from the edge.

7. Stitch, crossing over the dots.
8. Cut out the four pieces, using the triangles as the pattern.
9. Press the seams to the light/medium side.
10. Trim off the tips.

Making Four

1. Lay the pieces out in this order:
2. Flip the piece on the right to the piece on the left.
3. Match and pin the center seams.
4. Assembly-line sew.
5. Square to 6 1/2".

Sewing the Block Together

1. Lay out the pieces.
2. Sew the vertical rows.
3. Sew the horizontal rows.

Tumbleweed is the middle block in the third row.

Set aside until the September block is completed.

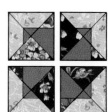

August

Enjoy the light sides of life.

Sunday	Monday	Tuesday	Wednesday

2 2/3 cups (7 oz) flaked coconut
2/3 cup sugar
6 Tbl flour
1/4 tsp salt

4 egg whites
1 tsp almond extract
1/2 tsp vanilla extract

Coconut Tumbleweeds
Debbie Smith

Combine coconut, sugar, flour and salt in a medium bowl. Stir in egg whites, almond extract and vanilla extract. Drop mixture by teaspoonful onto lightly greased baking sheet. Bake 325° 20 minutes or until edges are golden brown. Remove from pan immediately. Makes 2 1/2 dozen.

Thursday	Friday	Saturday

Tips

Air out your quilts, but don't beat them like rugs!

As certain as a young man's fancy, our fancy turns to thoughts of spring cleaning. To minimize color fading of your fabrics and quilts, use a phosphate free washing product. Store your quilts for the summer in an old pillow case. Never use plastic bags for storing them as plastic does not allow the fabric to breathe.
Nancy Loftis

Store your quilts as well as fabric away from sunlight to help protect from fading.

To Market, To Market

Intermediate block   made by Lucille Townsend

Choose a light,
two mediums,
and two darks.

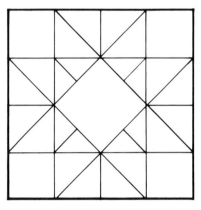

Create your own block.

Cutting Instructions

Layer Cut Right Sides Together

(1) 4" x 8" first medium
(1) 4" x 8" second medium
 4

(1) 4" x 8" light
(1) 4" x 8" first dark
 4

Cut

(4) 3 1/2" squares second dark
 4

(1) 4 7/8" square second dark
 1

Cut into Fourths on the Diagonal

(1) 4 1/2" square first medium
(1) 4 1/2" square first dark
 4

Making

Four

1. Draw on 4" square lines. Draw on diagonal lines. Pin.

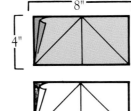

2. Sew a **1/4" seam** on both sides of the diagonal lines. Press.

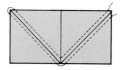

3. Cut apart on all lines.

4. Press the seams to the darker side.

5. Square to 3 1/2".

Making

Four

1. Lay out the four triangles.

2. Assembly-line sew.

3. Press the seam to the darker side.

4. Fold the 4 7/8" square into fourths and press .

5. Flip one piece right sides together to the large square, pin matching the centers. Allow tips to hang over equally.

6. Sew. Press seams away from the square.

7. Add the remaining three pieces to the square.

8. Square to 6 1/2".

Sewing

the Block

Together

1. Assembly-line sew the top and bottom rows. Clip the connecting threads.

3. Carefully match, pin, and sew side pieces to the center square.

2. Sew the side pieces together.

4. Sew the top and bottom rows to the center row.

To Market, To Market is the third block in the third row.

Sew together the blocks of the third row.

Turn to the back of the Almanac for instructions.

September

Sunday	Monday	Tuesday	Wednesday
☐	☐	☐	☐
☐	☐	☐	☐
☐	☐	☐	☐
☐	☐	☐	☐
☐	☐	☐	☐

1 lb link turkey sausages
2 eggs
1/2 tsp salt
1 cup sifted flour
1 cup milk

A Market Day Yorkshire Pudding

Joy Harvey

In an 8" square pan, brown sausage in a 425 ° oven. Drain off most of grease from pan, leaving enough to coat the pan. Pour batter over sausages. Bake until golden brown and puffy, 20-25 min. Serve at once.

Thursday	Friday	Saturday
☐	☐	☐
☐	☐	☐
☐	☐	☐
☐	☐	☐
☐	☐	☐

Tips

Make scrap quilts using fabrics left over from children's clothing. When grown, those children will associate happy times with the quilts.

What? You really believe you can make a quilt in a day?

To see the true color, take the fabric outside into the daylight away from artificial light.

If fabric bleeds while pre-washing, "set" the color by soaking it with 1/4 cup salt in the rinse cycle.

Pigs in a Blanket

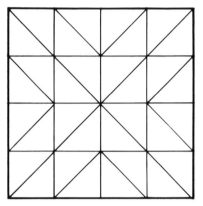

Intermediate block

made by Milly Warner

October

Choose a light,
medium,
and dark.

Create your own block.

Cutting Instructions

Layer Cut Right Sides Together

(1) 8" square light

(1) 8" square medium

 8

(1) 8" square light

(1) 8" square dark

 8

Making Eight

1. Draw on 4" square lines.

2. Draw on diagonal lines. Pin.

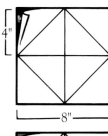

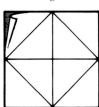

3. Sew a **1/4" seam** on both sides of the diagonal lines. Press.

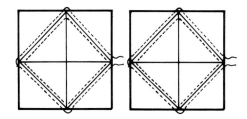

4. Cut apart on all lines.

5. Press the seams to the darker side.

6. Square to 3 1/2".

Sewing the Block Together

1. Lay out the pieces.

2. Sew the vertical rows.

3. Sew the horizontal rows.

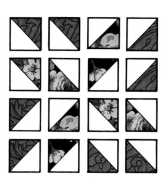

Variation: Block also known as Poinsettia in holiday colors.

Variation made by Ruth Hakala

Variation made by Linda Steiner

Pigs in a Blanket is the first block in the fourth row.

Set aside until the December block is completed.

October

Enjoy the bits and pieces of life.

Sunday	Monday	Tuesday	Wednesday

4 eggs
1 cup vegetable oil
3 cups sugar
2 cups pumpkin
2 cups wheat flour

1 cup white flour
2 tsp baking soda
1 tsp each salt, cinnamon,
    nutmeg and ginger
1 cup chopped walnuts

Pumpkin Bread
Lucina Heipt

Preheat oven to 350°. Grease and flour two loaf pans. Combine eggs, oil and sugar. Add pumpkin and blend. In separate bowl, combine dry ingredients, and stir into pumpkin batter until blended. Add nuts. Bake for one hour or until done.

Thursday	Friday	Saturday
☐	☐	☐
☐	☐	☐
☐	☐	☐
☐	☐	☐
☐	☐	☐

Tips

In preparation for layer-cutting and sewing, stack and press the fabrics right sides together on top of one another. Fabrics then stick together, and are ready for sewing!

When storing fabric strips in the middle of a project, drape them over a clothes hanger and clip them in place with a clothes pin.

Spools

November

Intermediate block

made by Luckie Yasukochi

Choose a light,
two mediums,
and two darks.

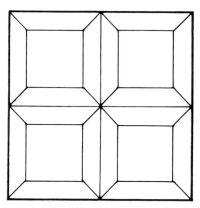

Create your own block.

Cutting Instructions

Layer Cut

(1) 3 5/8" square from each medium and dark

    1

(2) 2 1/8" x 6 5/8"strips from each medium and dark

  2

(16) 2 1/8" squares light

 16

(2) 2 1/8" x 15" strips light

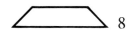 8

44

Making One of Each

1. Assembly-line sew the (4) 3 5/8" squares to one light strip.
2. Sew the second light strip to the opposite side.
3. Press the seams to the dark side.
4. Cut apart between the squares.

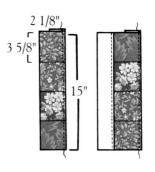

Making Two of Each

1. Draw a diagonal line on the wrong side of each 2 1/8" square.

2. Place a 2 1/8" square right sides to one end

of each 2 1/8 " x 6 5/8" strip.

3. Assembly-line sew all squares on the penciled diagonal line.

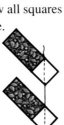

4. Place a 2 1/8" square right sides to the

opposite end of each strip .

5. Assembly-line sew on the penciled diagonal line.
6. Clip the threads holding them together. Trim away the excess light triangle and medium or dark triangle.

7. Open and press the seams to the darker side.

Making Four

1. Stack the pieces in color order.
2. Flip the narrow strip to the center piece. Match and pin at the dots 1/4" in.
3. Assembly-line sew the strips to both sides.
4. Press. Square to 6 1/2".

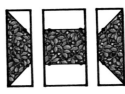

Sewing the Block Together

1. Lay out the pieces.
2. Sew the vertical row.
3. Sew the horizontal row.

Spools is the middle block in the fourth row.

Set aside until the December block is completed.

November

Sunday	Monday	Tuesday	Wednesday
☐	☐	☐	☐
☐	☐	☐	☐
☐	☐	☐	☐
☐	☐	☐	☐
☐	☐	☐	☐

1 cup flour
1/4 tsp salt
1 cup sugar
1 tsp baking powder

2 Tbl melted shortening
1 cup milk
1 cup nuts chopped
1 cup dates chopped

Date Pudding, a Sweet Holiday Dessert

Lucille Townsend

Mix all ingredients and pour into greased 10" square baking dish. Mix 1 1/4 cups **brown sugar** and 1 1/4 cups warm **water** together for syrup. Pour over top of pudding. (Do not mix.) Bake in moderate oven 350 ° until done, about 1 hr. Serve with **whipped cream**.

Tips

Get in the habit of closing your rotary cutter each time you lay it down.

Carry your rotary cutter in a spare eyeglasses case for its protection and yours!

Thursday	Friday	Saturday
☐	☐	☐
☐	☐	☐
☐	☐	☐
☐	☐	☐
☐	☐	☐

Christmas Star

December

Advanced block

made by Carmen Gil

Choose a light, medium, and two darks.

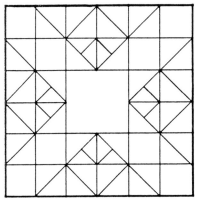

Create your own block.

Cutting Instructions

Layer Cut Right Sides Together

(1) 6" square light

(1) 6" square first dark
 8

(1) 6" square light

(1) 6" square medium
 8

(2) 3 1/2" squares light

(2) 3 1/2" squares medium
 4
4

Cut

(1) 4 1/2" square medium or dark
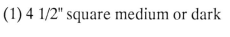 1

(8) 2 1/2" squares light
 8

Cut in Half on the Diagonal

(4) 3" squares second dark
 8

Making Eight	1. Draw on 3" square lines. 2. Draw on diagonal lines. Pin. 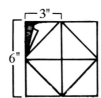	3. Sew a **1/4"** seam on both sides of the diagonal lines. Press. 4. Cut apart on all lines and press open. 5. Square to 2 1/2".
Making Four	1. Stack four of each in this order: 2. Assembly-line sew.	
Making Four	1. Draw on diagonal lines. Pin. 2. Sew **1/4" seam** on both sides of the diagonal lines. Press. 3. Cut into fourths. 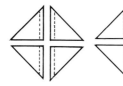	4. Press the seam to the darker side. 5. Stack four of each in this order: 6. Assembly-line sew. 7. Press the seams to the darker side. 8. Square to 2 1/2".
Making Four	1. Stack four of each in this order: 2. Assembly-line sew, carefully matching at seams.	
Sewing the Block Together	1. Lay out the pieces. 2. Sew the vertical rows. 3. Sew the horizontal rows.	

Christmas Star is the third block in the fourth row.

Sew together the fourth row. Turn to the back of the Almanac for instructions.

December

Sunday	Monday	Tuesday	Wednesday
☐	☐	☐	☐
☐	☐	☐	☐
☐	☐	☐	☐
☐	☐	☐	☐
☐	☐	☐	☐

1- 3 oz pkg lime gelatin
1 cup boiling water
8 oz can crushed pineapple,
    drain (save juice)

8 oz creamy cottage cheese
8 oz heavy whipping cream (whip)
1/2 cup mayonniase
1/4--1 cup walnuts, chopped

Emerald Christmas Salad
Dee McDaniel

Dissolve gelatin in boiling water. Add pineapple juice. Chill until slightly thickened. Beat until frothy. Fold in remaining ingredients. Chill until firm. 6 servings.

Thursday	Friday	Saturday
☐	☐	☐
☐	☐	☐
☐	☐	☐
☐	☐	☐
☐	☐	☐

Tips

It is essential to sew a quarter inch seam allowance. Quilts go together much easier!

Pat Wetzel

A magnetic seam guide, or a narrow strip of adhesive mole skin, placed at the edge or in front of the presser foot will assure a consistent seam allowance.

Resolve to never put a project away for the day with a mistake in it. Remove the mistake and then put it away. You are more likely to return to it.

Deborah Ward

Buy the best quality 100% cotton yardage for your quilts. They will last longer and retain their beauty longer.

Finishing Your Quilt

Checking Your Blocks

If any of the match points need improving, "unsew" with your rotary cutter. Hold it between the thumb and forefinger of your right hand and support it with your middle finger. Drop the blade against the stitches as you put tension on the two pieces of fabric, exposing the seam. Resew.

Check that each block is approximately 12 1/2" square. Straighten the outside edges if necessary without trimming away any of the 1/4" seam allowance.

• Do not be concerned if there is a slight variance in block sizes. If the blocks average slightly less than 12 1/2", trim the 12 1/2" lattice pieces to that measurement.

Choose one of the two different methods of finishing your quilt.

• Unquilted Blocks with Quick Turn and Tie Finish

• Quilted Blocks with Machine Quilted Finish

Quick Turn and Tie Finish

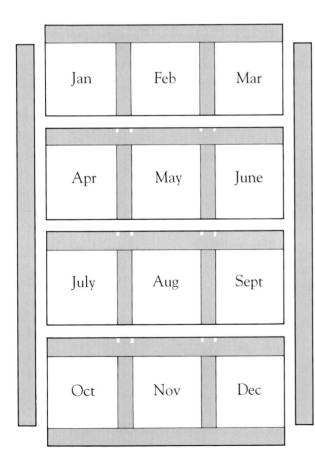

Sewing the Unquilted Blocks Together

Use this method if you are not going to machine quilt each individual block. Sew three blocks into rows quarterly.

1. Lay out rows of blocks in monthly chronological order with 12 1/2" lattice between them.

2. Sew together, stretching or easing each block to fit the lattice as you stitch.

3. Measure a row of sewn together blocks. Trim (5) 45" lattice strips to that measurement.

4. Pin and sew a long lattice strip to the top of each sewn together row. Sew a long strip to the bottom of the fourth row.

5. So that rows line up, extend lines from the 12 1/2" lattice strips and chalk mark on the long strips.

6. Pin-match the marked lattice to the lower edge of each row, and sew the rows together.

7. Piece the four remaining 45" lattice strips into two long strips. Measure, pin, and sew to the two long sides of the quilt.

Sewing the Borders to the Unquilted Top

1. Measure the width of the quilt. Cut two equal pieces.

2. Pin and stitch to the top and bottom.

3. Unfold, and measure the length, including the two borders.

4. Pin and sew the side borders.

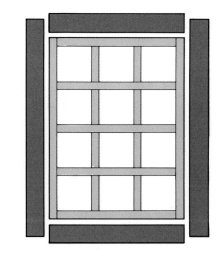

Quick Turning the Unquilted Top

1. Place the quilt right sides together to the backing.

2. Pin around the outside edge. Trim the excess backing.

3. Stitch around the outside edge, leaving a 15" opening in the middle of one side. Do not turn right side out.

4. Lay the bonded batting out flat. Place the quilt on top. Trim excess batting. Loosely stitch the layers together to the seam allowance.

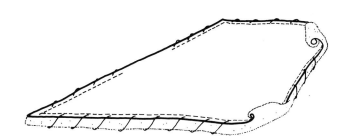

5. Station a person at each corner of the quilt. Begin rolling tightly in each corner and the sides toward the opening.

6. Open up the opening over this wad of fabric and batting, pop the quilt right side out through the hole, and carefully unroll with the layers together.

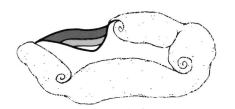

7. Working on opposite sides, grasp the edges of the quilt and pull in opposite directions to smooth out the batting.

8. Whipstitch the opening shut.

Tying Down the Unquilted Top

1. Smooth out the quilt on a table or large floor area.

2. Thread a curved needle with a long piece of all six strands of embroidery floss or pearl cotton for multiple tying.

3. Working from the center blocks out, take a stitch through all thicknesses in one corner of the block. Without clipping the threads, pull the floss to the next corner of the block, and take a stitch. Stitch all four corners with one continuous strand. *For more dimension, tie within the block.*

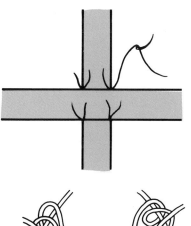

4. Clip the threads.

5. Take the floss on the right and wrap it twice around the floss on the left. Pull both pieces tight.

6. Take the floss on the left and wrap it twice around the floss on the right. Pull both pieces tight into a "surgeon's square knot."

7. Clip the strands to 1/2".

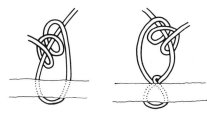

Surgeon's Square Knot

Borders can be "stitched in the ditch" for more dimension. See machine quilting techniques.

Machine Quilted Finish

Use this method if you are going to machine quilt blocks on rows of batting. Three blocks are machine quilted quarterly.

Cutting the Piece of Lightweight Bonded Batting

1. Cut the batting to the exact size of 63" x 81".

2. Leave the lightweight bonded batting in one large piece and cut off each row of batting as you need it.

Do not trim away the excess batting from the blocks. Additional batting is allowed around all outside edges for the borders. After the top is layered on the backing, the borders are added through all layers, and the quilt is finished with a straight piece of binding.

Machine Quilting Blocks in Rows to Batting

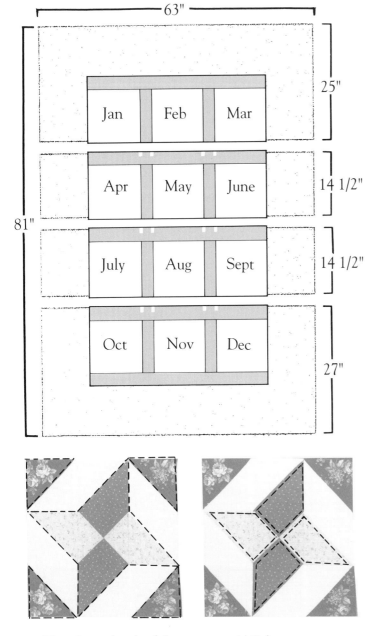

"Stitch in the ditch"   1/4" from seam

1. Place the February block on the 25" strip of batting in bottom center position. Let the edge of the block hang over 1/4". Pin in place. To manage the batting, roll the edges and safety pin in place.

2. Thread your machine with invisible thread. Loosen your top tension, and lengthen your stitch to 8-10 stitches per inch. Use walking foot.

3. Load your bobbin with neutral sewing thread.

4. Decide what pieces of the block to outline. "Stitch in the ditch" by placing the needle in the depth of the seam, and stitch. Backstitch. You may "machine quilt" by lining up the presser foot with the edge of the pieces, and stitch 1/4" away.

   If possible, stitch continuously without removing the block from under the needle, pivoting with the needle in the fabric at the points.

5. Pin a 12 1/2" lattice right sides together to each side of the block. Stitch through all thicknesses, and fold back.

6. Pin the January and March blocks right sides together to each lattice. Stitch, fold back and pin. "Stitch in the ditch, or machine quilt."

7. Measure the three blocks. Trim (5) 45" lattice strips to that measurement.

8. Sew a long lattice strip to the top of the row. The first three rows are sewn in this manner.

9. On the bottom row, long lattice strips are sewn to the top and bottom of the blocks. To allow room for the top long lattice strip, position the center block 2 1/2" down from the top of the batting.

Sewing the Machine Quilted Rows Together

The four rows of blocks quilted to the batting are now sewn together into one top.

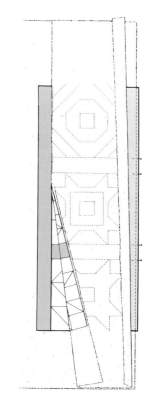

1. So that rows line up, extend lines from the 12 1/2" lattice strips and chalk mark on the long strips.

2. Place the second row right sides together to the first row. If necessary, snip the batting away from the edges, and fold back out of the way.

3. Match-pin the lattice. Stretch or ease each lattice marking to fit each block as you stitch.

4. Fold the two rows back and flat.

5. Trim away any excess batting, and pat flat.

6. Hand whipstitch the butted batting flat in place.

7. Add the remaining two rows in this manner.

Layering the Quilted Top on the Backing

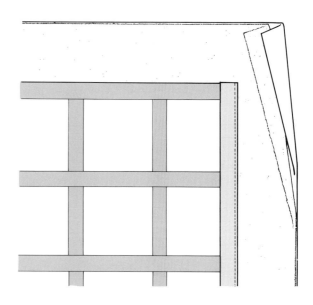

1. Spread out the backing on a large table or floor area with the right side down. Clamp the fabric to the edge of the table with binder clips, or tape the backing to the floor.

2. With the top right side up, center on the backing. Smooth until all layers are flat.

3. Safety pin the layers together through the lattice. Use a grapefruit spoon to assist pinning process.

4. Piece the remaining lattice strips. Measure the sides, and cut the lattice that measurement.

5. Pin the lattice right sides together to the sides through all thicknesses.

6. Use 10 stitches per inch, bobbin thread to match the backing, and a walking foot.

7. Stitch through all thicknesses.

8. Unfold both long lattice back and flat. Pin.

Sewing the Borders to the Quilted Top

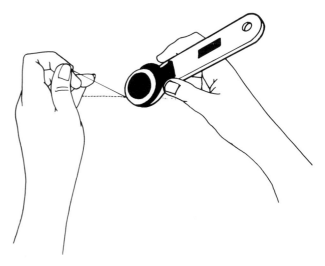

1. Measure the width of the quilt. Cut two equal pieces.

2. Pin and stitch to the top and bottom through all thicknesses.

3. Unfold, and measure the length, including the two borders.

4. Pin and sew the side borders.

If puckers appear on the backside, remove stitching by grasping the bobbin thread (with a tweezers) and pull gently to expose the invisible thread. Touch the invisible thread stitches with the rotary cutter blade as you pull the bobbin thread free from the quilt.

Adding the Binding

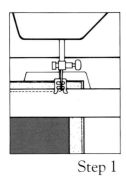

Step 1

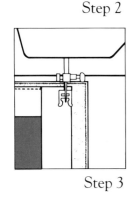

Step 2

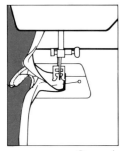

Step 3

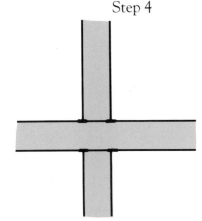

Step 4

Use a walking foot attachment and regular thread on top and in the bobbin to match the binding

1. Line up the raw edges of the folded binding with the raw edges of the quilt in the middle of one side.

2. Begin stitching 4" from the end of the binding.

3. At the corner, stop the stitching 1/4" from the edge with the needle in the fabric. Raise the presser foot and turn the quilt to the next side. Put the foot back down. Step 1

4. Stitch backwards 1/4" to the edge of the binding, raise the foot, and pull the quilt forward slightly.

5. Fold the binding strip straight up on the diagonal. Fingerpress in the diagonal fold. Step 2

6. Fold the binding strip straight down with the diagonal fold underneath. Line up the top of the fold with the raw edge of the binding underneath.

7. Begin sewing 1/4" in from the edge at the original pivot point. Step 3

8. Continue stitching and mitering the corners around the outside of the quilt.

9. Stop stitching 4" from where the ends will overlap.

10. Line up the two ends of binding. Trim the excess with a 1/2" overlap. Open out the folded ends and pin right sides together. Sew a 1/4" seam. Step 4

11. Continue to stitch the binding in place.

12. Trim the batting and backing up to the raw edges of the binding.

13. Fold the binding to the back side of the quilt. Pin in place so that the folded edge on the binding covers the stitching line. Tuck in the excess fabric at each miter on the diagonal.

14. From the right side, "stitch in the ditch" using invisible thread on the right side, and a bobbin thread to match the binding on the back side. Catch the folded edge of the binding on the back side with the stitching.

Anchoring the Body of the Quilt

Hold the quilt top together to the backing with embroidery floss and surgeon's square knots (see Surgeon's Square Knot illustration), machine quilting through all lattice, or with bar tacks.

Bar Tacking the Quilt to the Backing (Optional)

1. At each corner of each block, place the needle in the depth of the seam, and stitch back and forth 1/4" several times.

2. Clip the threads.